JUMP!

TREE FROGS

Lynette Robbins

PowerKiDS
press.
New York

For Emily

Published in 2012 by The Rosen Publishing Group, Inc.
29 East 21st Street, New York, NY 10010

First Edition

Editor: Joanne Randolph
Book Design: Ashley Drago and Erica Clendening

Photo Credits: Cover, pp. 4, 8, 11 (top), 14, 16, 18–19, 22 Shutterstock.com; p. 5 © www.iStockphoto.com/Craig Veltri; pp. 6, 9 (bottom) © www.iStockphoto.com/Brandon Alms; p. 7 Joel Sartore/Getty Images; p. 9 (top) © www.iStockphoto.com/Adrian Matthiassen; p. 10 Danita Delimont/Getty Images; p. 11 (bottom) © www.iStockphoto.com/Sebastian Duda; pp. 12–13 Gail Shumway/Getty Images; pp. 15 (top), 20 iStockphoto/Thinkstock; p. 15 (bottom) © www.iStockphoto.com/Mark Kostich; p. 17 Daly and Newton/Getty Images; p. 21 © www.iStockphoto.com/Kerstin Klaassen.

Library of Congress Cataloging-in-Publication Data

Robbins, Lynette.
 Tree frogs / by Lynette Robbins. — 1st ed.
     p. cm. — (Jump!)
 Includes index.
 ISBN 978-1-4488-5017-4 (library binding) — ISBN 978-1-4488-5167-6 (pbk.) — ISBN 978-1-4488-5168-3 (6-pack)
 1. Hylidae—Juvenile literature. I. Title.
 QL668.E24R63 2012
 597.87'8—dc22

2011004915

Manufactured in the United States of America

CPSIA Compliance Information: Batch #WS11PK: For Further Information contact Rosen Publishing, New York, New York at 1-800-237-9932

Contents

Hello to You, Tree Frog!

Frogs live in or near the water, right? This is true of many frogs. You may be surprised to learn that some frogs live in trees, though. There are many kinds of tree frogs that spend most of their lives hopping from branch to branch, high in the treetops.

Just like all frogs, tree frogs are **amphibians**. Salamanders and newts are

Red-eyed tree frogs are one of the best-known kinds of tree frogs. They live in rain forests in southern Mexico, Central America, and northern South America.

also amphibians. Amphibians spend part of their lives in the water and part on land. Even though they live in trees as adults, tree frogs spend the beginnings of their lives in the water, as tadpoles. Most amphibians have moist skin. They do not need to drink water because they soak it up through their skin.

Here a group of tree frogs rest together on a tree trunk. They have sticky toes that help them hang on to branches and tree trunks.

Home, Hopping Home

Tree frogs live on almost every **continent**. Many tree frogs live in Central and South America. Tree frogs also live in North America, Europe, Australia, and some parts of Asia and Africa.

Many kinds of tree frogs live in warm, tropical rain forests. Some kinds of tree frogs live in **temperate** forests. Some kinds of tree frogs do not even live in trees at all! They

This is a clown tree frog. Clown tree frogs live in wet forests or swamps in Bolivia, Brazil, Colombia, Ecuador, Venezuela, and Peru.

live on the ground. Most ground-dwelling tree frogs live near ponds, marshes, or streams. Some ground-dwelling tree frogs live in dry places. They dig burrows to keep themselves safe from the hot sun.

This tree frog makes its home in a swamp in Arkansas.

Tons of Tree Frogs

There are more than 700 different kinds of tree frogs. Most tree frogs would easily fit in the palm of your hand. They are small and light so that they can hop on branches and leaves without breaking them.

Tree frogs can be hard to find. Most are green or brown to blend in with the trees. Some tree frogs have patches

Blanchard's tree frog has bumpy skin with patches of brown, green, or gray on it. These markings help it blend in on the banks of the slow-moving streams where it lives.

of bright colors. Others have bright colors on their legs that show only when they are jumping. **Predators** may be confused to see a flash of color on a jumping frog. Then the frog can find a new hiding spot, where it can blend in once again.

ABOVE: This green tree frog's coloring helps it blend in with its leafy resting spot. Green tree frogs are common frogs in North America.

RIGHT: The red-eyed tree frog has bright colors that it uses to surprise enemies. It keeps its colors hidden as it rests and then flashes them to make its getaway.

9

Jumping and Climbing

Tree frogs generally walk or climb. Tree frogs have long legs and large feet to help with these activities. They have sticky pads on the ends of their fingers and toes. These pads help them hold tightly on to branches, leaves, and bark. The skin on their bellies also helps

It is easy to see the sticky toe pads on this tree frog. They are the round, white parts on its feet.

them stick to tree trunks and branches. Many tree frogs have webbed hands and feet, but not all of them do.

Most tree frogs hop only to get away from predators. Some tree frogs also hop when they are hunting. When they do jump, their long legs help them go far, though!

LEFT: This tree frog stretches out its fingers and toes as it jumps. The webbing between its fingers and toes helps it stay in the air a bit longer than it would otherwise.

ABOVE: Red-eyed tree frogs and other tree frogs can climb high into treetops or hang upside down under leaves using their sticky toes.

Tree Frog Facts

Tree frogs are **nocturnal**. That means that they are most active at night.

5

Male frogs sometimes take turns croaking. One frog croaks while the other frog rests or hunts for food.

3

A tree frog's eyes are on the sides of its head, rather than on the top, as a frog that lives in the water's eyes are.

4

When a male frog croaks, its throat fills up with air the way a balloon does. This helps make the croak louder so that females will hear it.

2

Many kinds of tree frogs can change the color of their skin to blend in with their environment.

1

Some kinds of tree frogs are kept as pets. They can live up to 16 years in **captivity**.

6

Some kinds of frogs are used for medicine. People use the **mucus** from White's tree frogs to heal skin sores.

7

Some frogs can live in very cold places. Gray tree frogs **hibernate** during the winter. Their bodies freeze solid. In the springtime, they thaw and hop away!

8

Water-holding tree frogs live in Australia's deserts. These frogs take in huge amounts of water through their skin. The water makes them swell to twice their normal size.

9

Aboriginal people sometimes dig up water-holding frogs for their water. They squeeze the water out of the frog and then let the frog go.

10

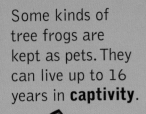

13

Dinnertime

How would you like to eat flies and ants for your dinner? Tree frogs eat all kinds of insects, as well as spiders, slugs, worms, and centipedes. A few kinds of tree frogs eat larger animals such as lizards and other frogs.

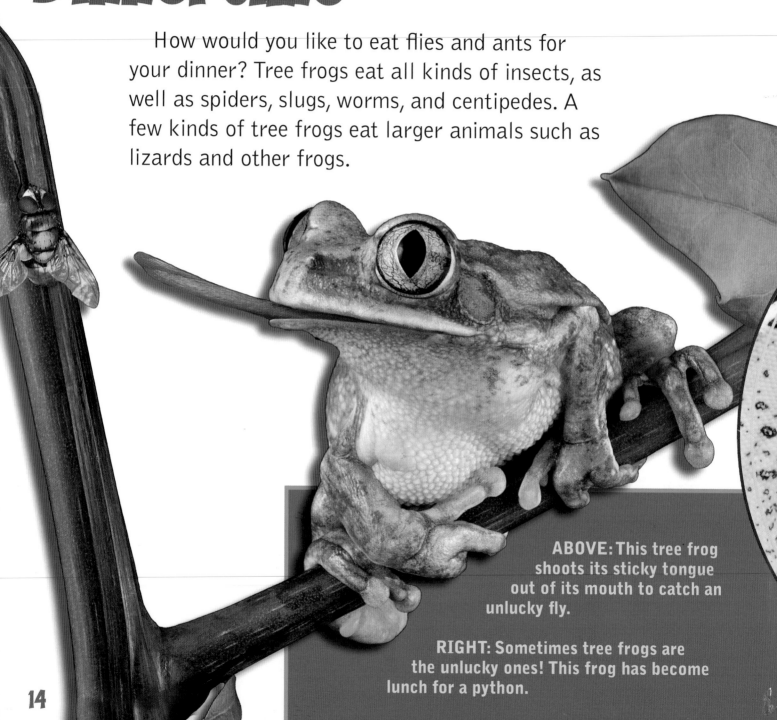

ABOVE: This tree frog shoots its sticky tongue out of its mouth to catch an unlucky fly.

RIGHT: Sometimes tree frogs are the unlucky ones! This frog has become lunch for a python.

Tree frogs are sometimes caught in spiderwebs, as this one has been.

Most tree frogs hunt at night. When an insect comes close enough, the tree frog catches it with its long, sticky tongue. Some tree frogs jump high into the air to catch their **prey**. Tree frogs must watch out for predators. Birds, snakes, lizards, and **rodents** all eat tree frogs. Some predators do not like the way tree frogs taste, though, so they do not hunt them.

The Dumpy Tree Frog

White's tree frog is a large tree frog. It can reach 4.5 inches (11 cm) in length. It sometimes has folds of fat on its head and back. This has given it the nickname the dumpy tree frog.

White's tree frog lives in a part of Australia where there are two seasons, a rainy season and a dry season.

White's tree frog has pupils that go across its eyes, instead of up and down as most other tree frogs' pupils do.

In the rainy season, White's tree frogs live in the trees. During the dry season, they cover themselves in mucus and dead skin. The covering keeps their bodies wet. Then they burrow into the ground to wait for the rainy season to come again.

Here you can see the folds of fat that give this tree frog its nickname.

Calling for a Mate

Have you ever heard a group of croaking frogs? A male frog croaks to help it find a female with which to **mate**. It also croaks to tell other male frogs to stay away. Frogs come together during the breeding season. This means that many male frogs can be heard croaking at once.

Different kinds of frogs croak in different ways. Male frogs may whistle, buzz, groan, or click. There may be many different kinds of frogs at a breeding site. The different calls help the females find males of their own kind with which to mate. Females like males with loud, strong croaks the best.

Male tree frogs make their loud calls by puffing up their throats.

Tadpole Time

Most female tree frogs lay their eggs in ponds, puddles, ditches, or streams. Some lay their eggs in water in large cup-shaped plants or in holes in trees. Others lay their eggs on leaves that hang over water. When the eggs hatch, the tiny tadpoles fall into the water.

Tree frog eggs take only a few days to hatch. Tree frog tadpoles are

Here many frog eggs are fixed to the underside of a leaf. Soon the new frogs will drop into the water.

herbivores. They eat algae and small plants. They start to grow arms and legs. They also lose their tails. Soon they will have turned into small tree frogs. Then they are ready to climb or hop out of the water and start living in the trees!

This tadpole has started to grow arms and legs. Its tail will get smaller over time until the frog is ready to leave the water.

Tree Frogs in Trouble

Even though tree frogs have many predators, their biggest danger comes from people. When people cut down forests to build farms, factories, and cities, they destroy tree frogs' **habitats**. Pollution also hurts tree frogs. Many kinds of tree frogs have become **endangered**. Tree frogs are also in danger from a disease that hurts their skin. Many frogs have died of this disease.

These two young frogs count on their forest home to keep them alive. Can you imagine a world where there were no more singing tree frogs?

Some people are trying to save these frogs by breeding them in captivity. Scientists are working hard to find a cure. Tree frogs are interesting animals. People need to help keep them from disappearing from our planet.

Glossary

Aboriginal (a-buh-RIJ-nul) Having to do with the first people to live in Australia.

amphibians (am-FIH-bee-unz) Animals that spend the first parts of their lives in water and the rest on land.

captivity (kap-TIH-vih-tee) A place where animals live, such as in a home, a zoo, or an aquarium, instead of living in the wild.

continent (KON-teh-nent) One of Earth's seven large landmasses.

endangered (in-DAYN-jerd) In danger of no longer existing.

habitats (HA-buh-tats) The surroundings where animals or plants naturally live.

herbivores (ER-buh-vorz) Animals that eat only plants.

hibernate (HY-bur-nayt) To spend the winter in a sleeplike state.

mate (MAYT) To come together to make babies.

mucus (MYOO-kus) A thick, slimy liquid produced by the bodies of many animals.

nocturnal (nok-TUR-nul) Active during the night.

predators (PREH-duh-terz) Animals that kill other animals for food.

prey (PRAY) An animal that is hunted by another animal for food.

rodents (ROH-dents) Animals with gnawing teeth, such as mice.

temperate (TEM-puh-rut) Not too hot or too cold.

Index

Web Sites

Due to the changing nature of Internet links, PowerKids Press has developed an online list of Web sites related to the subject of this book. This site is updated regularly. Please use this link to access the list:
www.powerkidslinks.com/jump/treefrog/

Withdrawn